Under His Wings

Emptiness

Looking to God in the Dry and Weary Times of Our Lives

(A Study of Psalm 63)

Written by Susan M. Schulz

Edited by Martha Streufert Jander

Editorial assistant: Laura Christian

3558 South Jefferson Avenue, St. Louis, MO 63118-3968
Manufactured in the United States of America

Contents

Session 1

David's Dry and Weary Time

Where Are We Going?

We will search the Scriptures to see the cause of David's emptiness and of our own. We will grow in understanding of Psalm 63, thereby making it an expression of our own emptiness and a source of confidence in how God can fill us with His mercy and love.

Ready, Set, Go

Begin with prayer, asking for the power of the Holy Spirit to lead you through this study so that God will fill you with His peace as He assures you of His presence.

Spend a few moments on "**Where Am I Now?**" briefly discussing the dryness of your life at the present time. Then, as you do "**The Search,**" look for God's message to you. God is reaching out to fill your emptiness. Write your answers in the space provided.

Take time to "**Respond,**" seeking God's answers in the psalm for your dry and weary times. Pray with and for each other, addressing any concerns shared during your study today.

Before the next session, do the "**Do,**" using the journal page and prayer starters following this lesson.

Where Am I Now?

Describe a time in your life when you experienced a physical thirst.

How would you describe the dryness of your life at the present time?

___ I'm up to my knees in sand.

___ Even my cactus plants are dying.
___ Desert winds are wailing all around me, but I have shelter.
___ Drop by drop, my thirst is being quenched.
___ One day the hot winds blow; the next day I feel the gentle rain.
___ I'm swimming in the pool of the oasis.

The Search

David's Dry and Weary Land

David wrote Psalm 63 while fleeing for his life from his son Absalom. For years he had neglected his family. Now those years were taking their toll in a most devastating way. David had become furious when Tamar, his daughter, was raped by her half brother, but he had done nothing. When Absalom killed that half brother, David shunned Absalom but did nothing to bring him to repentance or to justice. For three years Absalom lived in exile; then for two more years he lived in Jerusalem without seeing the king (2 Samuel 14:28). And for four more years Absalom plotted the king's overthrow, sitting by the gate of the city and giving advice to those who came seeking the king's justice. Yet again, David did nothing to reprimand Absalom or to get him to see his sins. Now Absalom's plotting was coming to fruition, and David had to flee.

1. David found himself not only in the dry and weary desert of Judah but also in a dry and weary emptiness in his life. Read 2 Samuel 15:13–17, 23–30 to get a better idea of David's situation. What were the outcomes of David's neglect of and leniency with Absalom?

2. Keeping David's circumstances in mind, slowly and meditatively read aloud David's cry to God in Psalm 63. Discuss David's feelings at the beginning of the psalm. Reread verses 1–2, taking note of David's use of word pictures to describe his thoughts and feelings. How does David describe his longing for God?

3. Events or circumstances in our lives can lead us into a dry and weary wilderness. We may draw away from God into our own selfishness. We may balk at facing our own sin. We may grieve about other people's sins against us. We may neglect worship and the Word and sacraments. What circumstances can cause desert effects? Why do you think that even Christians wander into the dry and weary wilderness? When have you had such experiences? How did you respond to the dry and weary times?

4a. Reread verses 2–3 of Psalm 63. What might David have remembered of his experiences in the sanctuary (tabernacle)? (See Psalm 27:4–6 for help.) How did the memory of his experiences affect his outlook? What was his response (Psalm 63:4) to his change of heart? Why do you think David's outlook changed?

4b. If you were unable to worship in God's house, what would you miss? How would your faith be affected? What memories of worship in God's house would bring comfort and the reassurance of God's love?

God's Quenching

5. God filled David's emptiness. David had sinned, but he also knew God as a loving and forgiving Savior. The knowledge of God's love, mercy, and forgiveness helped David to rejoice in God. Reread verses 5–8 and notice the rich language David uses to express his change of heart. Record some of those here.

6. God has not changed. He reaches out to us in love, mercy, and forgiveness. He comes to us in His saving Word and at His altar, offering us the evidence of His love in the body and blood of our Lord Jesus Christ. He longs to fill us with His peace, love, and joy. Take heart in knowing that God can and does fill your emptiness because, like David, you belong to Him in Jesus. David believed in the promised Savior, and we have seen the fulfillment of that promise. The book of Hebrews assures us (6:19) that "we have this hope as an anchor for the soul, firm and secure." Reflect on the hope you have in the love and forgiveness God offers. What can you remember about God that will help you in your "desert times"?

Respond

The Lord led David from dry, weary emptiness to joyful expectation of His fulfilling love and mercy. As children of God, we use Psalm 63 to express our own emptiness to God, honestly and openly. We remember and think deeply about the past evidences of God's power, glory, and love. We praise God for all He has done and all that He will do, being confident that He does care for us and will fill us with His love.

Pair up with a partner and read the psalm to each other, substituting your partner's name for the "I" and "my" words in the psalm and for "the king" in verse 11.

Pray together in your large group, gently encouraging one another to participate. Pray with and for each other, addressing any of the concerns you shared during your study today.

Do

This week pay attention to the situations in your life in which you find yourself dry, weary, and empty. Summarize those experiences in your journal pages. Use word pictures to describe your situation. Ask the Lord to help you recognize the causes of your "desert times," confess your need of Him and His love, and open you to His joy and love. Change may happen, though it may happen slowly. But be assured that, no matter how dry and weary we are, God's peace and His presence are real. His promises do not fail.

Additional readings for this week: Psalm 61; Isaiah 43; and 1 John 3:20. Copy and attach to a mirror or other place you see daily the words of 2 Corinthians 1:20.

Use the prayer starters each day as you come to the Lord in your quiet time, either writing in your own endings to the sentences or leaving them blank to be used in a new way each day.

For next week, read Ruth. Also read through and think about Session 2, filling in before class any responses as you like.

Journal Page

O Lord, You are so

and I am so

Please forgive me for

Help me

Please bless and take care of

Thanks, Lord, for

Session 2

Naomi's Times of Emptiness

Where Are We Going?

In this session, we will come to realize the faithfulness of God and how He comes to us when we, like Naomi, respond to emptiness in sinful ways. We will see that while our sin has consequences, God faithfully leads us to repentance, forgives our sin, and fills us with His love.

Ready, Set, Go

Begin with prayer, asking God to bless your study of His Word and help you grow in confidence of His steadfast love.

Take a look at "**Where Am I Now?**" and briefly discuss the questions there. As you do "**The Search**," discover God's faithfulness to Naomi and to you. Write your answers in the spaces provided.

Take time to "**Respond**," recognizing God's power and love at work in your life and responding to God's faithful love in prayer.

Before the next session, do the "**Do**," using the journal page and prayer starters following this lesson.

Where Am I Now?

Share a childhood experience of being alone, lost, in a strange place, or with people you did not know. Do you remember what your feelings were? How did you react?

The Search

Empty Responses

Emptiness in Judah (famine) caused Naomi and her family to leave their homeland to live as foreigners in Moab. Perhaps in a strange country among foreign people, perhaps with few friends or fellow Israelites, Naomi already experienced some emptiness.

1. After some time in this strange country, Naomi's husband died and left her with her two sons—and more emptiness. The sons grew up and married young Moabite women. Although such marriages were not at that time forbidden by law, how might they have added to Naomi's emptiness?

2a. Then Naomi's sons died—and her sons' wives were childless. Her emptiness couldn't get any emptier. As a group, read aloud Ruth 1 to discover Naomi's responses to her emptiness. Look especially at verses 13 and 20–21. How does Naomi view God in her situation? How is her view of God different from David's in Psalm 63? How does Naomi's outlook affect her relationship with God and her sense of emptiness?

2b. Oftentimes when we face emptiness, our sinful nature urges us to respond in detrimental ways, but sinful responses to emptiness are merely a slippery slope to the very bottom of the pit. Discuss some of the responses that follow. Maybe you even noted some of these in your journal this past week. (You do not need to share these, unless you wish to do so.) What effect do these responses have on our emptiness? What blessings from

God can be short-circuited because of these responses?
Lash out
Lock it all inside and pretend you're fine
Sigh and mope a lot
Reject all offers of help, concern, and compassion
Try to fill the emptiness by doing "stuff"
Reject God
Allow the devil to convince you that God doesn't love you
Sink into complete hopelessness and despair
Other: ______________________________

3. Sometimes we are so busy complaining and blaming God that we do not see—and might even reject—the blessings God is working in our lives—often through the love of those around us. Why did Naomi so persistently reject Ruth's desire to help? Why do we reject others' help and concern?

Faithful Forgiveness and Love

When we respond sinfully, we need but one thing—God's merciful forgiveness in Christ Jesus. When God convicts us of rejecting Him and those He sends to help us, we fall to our knees in repentance. Our Lord never turns us away. He is faithful even when we act faithlessly. Naomi's lack of faith left her lacking. Our lack of faith leaves us lacking too. Our God, however, never leaves us alone in our emptiness. He is faithful.

4. God keeps on being faithful. He does not turn His back on us, nor does He leave us on our own even when we insist on going our own way. Read the following verses, then discuss and record God's faithfulness to Naomi in spite of her sinful responses:

Ruth 1:22 ______________________________

Ruth 2:17–20 ____________________________

Ruth 4:9–10 ____________________________

Ruth 4:13–17 ____________________________

5a. God never quit working His wonderful plan on Naomi's behalf. Naomi's complaints didn't stop Him or His love, but only left her with a lack of peace and hope. His love seemed hidden to Naomi, but it was always there, always doing what was best for her, always working to fill her gnawing emptiness. How might the words of Psalm 63 have helped Naomi to see God's faithful love in her life?

5b. Recall and discuss times God showed His faithful love in the lives of other Bible characters even when they acted faithlessly (though not in unbelief).

5c. Share times in your own life when God was faithful in spite of your unfaithfulness. (If you wish, do this in the quietness of your own heart.)

6. God's love can fill us as it filled Naomi. As you look at Psalm 63 again, jot down and discuss phrases that make you sure of God's love for you and God's peace and presence in your life.

Respond

Verse 2 of Psalm 63 shows David's confidence that God's power was at work in his life. God assures us, also, of His constant power and love, just as He was faithfully at work in Naomi's life. God's Law convicts us of our sin. God's love works repentance in our hearts. God forgives us and helps us yield to His plan. *He* changes us through His faithful, forgiving love.

Hold hands with one or two others while saying the words of Psalm 63:1–8 together; if needed, also speak words of encouragement and forgiveness to one another. Then ponder God's faithfulness for one quiet minute before joining in the closing prayer.

In your group prayers, respond to God's faithful love for you. Praise Him for His faithfulness. Ask for eyes to see His daily grace and mercy. Pray with and for each other, addressing any concerns shared during your study today.

Do

This week pay attention to the various ways you react to emptiness. Also look back on your responses in the past. In your journal, make a note of and evaluate these responses. Did they cause you to slide deeper into the pit of emptiness? Write a prayer of confession, asking God to forgive you for responding to emptiness by turning away from Him and those He has provided to help. Ask for the Holy Spirit to open your eyes to what God is doing and has done to show His faithful love.

Soak yourself in God's love through His Word: Ephesians 3:16–21; Psalm 145:13–21; Psalm 146; Psalm 33. Write the words of 2 Timothy 2:13 on a card. Tape it to your mirror or on the refrigerator as a constant reminder of God's faithfulness.

Fill in the prayer page and pray the prayers each day during your devotion time.

For next week, read through and think about Session 3, filling in answers as you wish.

Journal Page

O Lord, You are so

and I am so

Please forgive me for

Help me

Please bless and take care of

Thanks, Lord, for

Session 3

Hannah, Remembered by God

In this lesson, we will look at God's use of emptiness for our eternal good and for His glory. We will realize more fully what fulfillment actually is and the true source of that fulfillment.

Ready, Set, Go

Begin with prayer, thanking God for His faithful love and asking Him to guide and bless your study of His Word. Ask for His Holy Spirit to open your eyes to how God uses our emptiness to fulfill His purpose for our lives.

Take a look at "**Where Am I Now?**" and briefly discuss causes of emptiness—especially the root cause of all emptiness, sin. Do "**The Search**" to grow in understanding of God's eternal purpose for Hannah and for you. Use the spaces provided for your answers.

Take time to "**Respond**" to God's faithful working in your life by praying for and speaking a blessing to each other.

Before the next session, do the "**Do,**" using the journal page and prayer starters following this lesson.

Where Am I Now?

As you look back on your life, what has caused you to feel dry, weary, and empty?

____ Death of a loved one
____ Illness
____ An unfulfilled want or need

____ Hurt and betrayal
____ Comparing yourself to others
____ Unsure of your niche
____ Failure (your own or of someone you were depending on)
____ Life changes (birth of a child, job change, children leaving home, moving)
____ Others________________________________

The Search

Hannah's Emptiness

1. Read aloud 1 Samuel 1:1–8. Briefly discuss Hannah's situation. Which of the causes listed in "Where Am I Now?" contributed to Hannah's emptiness? What (and who) made things worse? How did Elkanah, Hannah's husband, try to console Hannah?

2. Elkanah's consolation was not enough to fill Hannah's aching soul. Hannah knew that only God could truly understand and help. Read 1 Samuel 1:9–18. Notice that in these verses no change occurs in Hannah's life situation, but Hannah herself changes dramatically. In what ways did Hannah change? Consider what role trust and a mature faith must have played.

Causes of Emptiness

3a. Discuss the importance and benefits of a strong faith relationship with God in our times of emptiness. Through what means does God strengthen our faith?

3b. How will a poorly fed faith lead to or increase emptiness? Why?

When our schedule and habits don't include feeding our faith through daily Bible reading, prayer, and regular participation in worship and the Lord's Supper, *we lose much of the peace and strength that God has for us.* When we realize our loss, we humbly and sincerely repent of our sin. God gives us His full forgiveness and uses *His* power to change us—including our tendency to neglect His Word.

The Cure for Emptiness

4. Dry and empty times may always be part of our lives here on earth. Our comfort is knowing that because God loves us and always does what is best for us, He even uses emptiness for our good and for His glory—and for the good of His kingdom (Hannah's son Samuel became one of God's great prophets). Remembering that God's goal for us is eternal life with Him in heaven, read more of Hannah's story in 1 Samuel 1:19–28 and 2:18–21. What effect do you think the Lord's closing of Hannah's womb for many years, and His later blessing of children, had on the faith life of Hannah, Elkanah, Eli, and maybe even Peninnah?

5. In Psalm 63 we also see God using David's emptiness for a purpose. Look at the psalm again and discuss the eternal benefits and the good for God's kingdom that God worked in David during his time of emptiness. What words and phrases beautifully show David's grasp of all that the Lord was doing for him?

6. Sometimes when we're empty, we look only for God's filling of our lives with earthly blessings. God's vision, however, is eternal. He is faithful to fill us, not necessarily in the way that we expect or desire, but in the way that is best for our eternal salvation and at times for the benefit of His kingdom. He may not change our situation, but may choose instead to transform us.

Emptiness for God's children always has a purpose—at times to bring us to repentance, always to strengthen our faith and to help us witness of His love and faithfulness to those around us. Emptiness is an opportunity to focus on Jesus, to remember His love—a love so great that He would empty Himself and die for us (Philippians 2:6–8). Share with the group, as you feel comfortable, a time in your life when God used emptiness for your good and for His glory and/or for the good of His kingdom. Or, in a general way, share what good you think God has accomplished through all the empty times in your life—especially for your eternal good and for the growth and good of His kingdom.

Respond

As you close today, take turns praying out loud the following prayer for the person on your right. If the person you are praying for has mentioned any other needs during today's session, add those to your prayer.

Dear Lord Jesus, thank You for ________________. Please, Lord, strengthen ______________'s faith through Your powerful Word. In times of emptiness, help ______________ to remember Your great love for her and that You are always working for her good and for the good of Your kingdom. In Your name we pray. Amen.

Then, all together read the following blessing to each other:

Remember the God you have—the God who sent Jesus to die for you. The God who controls every situation. The God who has been faithful in the past. The God who will use every emptiness of the present and future for His good purpose. The God whose love for you endures forever.

Do

Look again at the list under "Where Am I Now?" Describe in your journal times God has used emptiness to bring you to repentance, to strengthen your faith, and/or to witness of His love and faithfulness to others. Look for and rejoice in God's faithfulness to you in years past. And look for and rejoice in God's faithfulness during this week.

Use the prayer starters each day as you come to the Lord in your quiet time, either writing your own endings to the sentences or leaving them blank to be used in a new way each day.

Use the following readings to feed your faith this week: Psalm 25; Psalm 136; Philippians 2:1–11. Write the words to Psalm 16:11 on a piece of paper and attach it where you will see it often.

For next week, read through and think about Lesson 4, filling in any responses as you like.

Journal Page

O Lord, You are so

and I am so

Please forgive me for

Help me

Please bless and take care of

Thanks, Lord, for

Session 4

The Empty Soul Filled with God's Love

Where Are We Going?

In this session, we will grow in our understanding of Psalm 63 and of God's all-encompassing love. We will look to God as the only true source of all fulfillment.

Ready, Set, Go

Begin with prayer, thanking God for His faithful love and asking Him to guide and bless your study of His Word. Ask for the presence of the Spirit as you seek what He is giving to you and doing through you.

Take a look at "**Where Am I Now?**" and briefly discuss the various sources we often look to for fulfillment. As you do "**The Search,**" seek a deeper understanding of Psalm 63 and its relevance and application to your life. Write your answers in the spaces provided.

Joyfully "**Respond**" to God's abundant love with prayer and praise.

Wrap up this study by doing the "**Do.**" Use the journal pages and prayer starters following this lesson.

Where Am I Now?

Remember the song line "looking for love in all the wrong places"? As Christians, we often do just that. We go looking for love, satisfaction, and security in all the wrong places. Make a list of some of the things we mistakenly look to for fulfillment (peace, security, happiness, love); discuss.

The Wrong Places List

Pause now to individually consider which of those listed is particularly tempting for you.

The Search

A Deeper Look at Psalm 63

1a. Read Psalm 63:1. In this verse, David not only vividly expresses his emptiness, he also expresses his greatest need in his time of emptiness. What is that need?

1b. How would you express your greatest need?

2a. Read verses 2–4. In the past when David experienced a longing for God, he knew where to go—to the sanctuary. There he realized the power of God to help him. There he experienced God's love. As David reflects on this previous fulfillment in the sanctuary, he reexperiences God's faithful, fulfilling love, which floods his thirsting soul. The experience is so powerful it changes the tone of his psalm and the rest of his life—"I will praise You *as long as I live.*"

Think back to Naomi and Hannah. How did their lives change when they realized God's great unfailing love for them?

2b. Talk about times when you experience God's love flooding your soul. Do times of emptiness often precede these experiences? How does realizing God's great love all over again leave a mark on your life?

3. Read verses 5–8. Choose one or two of the verses you just read and share with the group why that particular verse best expresses the mark of God's love on your life.

4. Read verses 9–11. David is still expressing the mark of God's love on his life. He is confident that God's will will be done. Those seeking power and fulfillment apart from God will receive the ultimate emptiness. Those who put their trust in God will receive the ultimate fulfillment—heaven. Why can you know this is true? How can focusing on your ultimate and eternal fulfillment strengthen you to make it through the dry and weary times of this life?

The True Source of Fulfillment

5a. Like David, we too need to realize that when we are empty, whether it is because of our own sin or other circumstances, there is only one true source of fulfillment. How has Psalm 63 and the four sessions of this Bible study helped you to realize God as the source of all peace, hope, security, love, and contentment?

5b. Knowing that God is the true source of fulfillment and that He fills us through intimate fellowship with Him, why is it so important that we feed our faith through regular worship, prayer, Bible study, and participation in the Lord's Supper?

6. Verse 11 reads, "But the king will rejoice in God; all who swear by God's name will praise Him." When God has filled your emptiness, what has been your response? How do you rejoice in God? How do you praise Him?

Respond

Fellowship with God brings again the realization of His faithful love for us. It changes our very lives. We have a joy and contentment that begs to be expressed with jubilant praise and confident hope. Enjoy a time of fellowship with God right now as you read together Ephesians 3:16–21.

How has the study of David, Naomi, Hannah, and especially Psalm 63 helped you "grasp how wide and long and high and deep is the love of Christ" for you? Reflect on your journalings over the past few weeks as you respond.

Praise and thank God in prayer (and song if you wish) for His deep love for you—especially the love that sent Jesus to die for you. Pray also that God will help you to be faithful in worship and the study of His Word. Be sure to include prayers for any concerns mentioned by the group today.

Do

This week use your journal page to write about and explore your own search for fulfillment. Where do you look for love? What do you think brings contentment? Is peace only possible when life is calm and easy? What makes you feel secure? As you consider your answers to these questions, confess to God the times you have looked in all the wrong places for fulfillment and ask Him to fill you with His forgiving love. Also spend some

time writing about the mark God's faithful love has left and is leaving on your life.

Use the prayer starters each day as you come to the Lord in your quiet time, either writing your own endings to the sentences or leaving them blank to be used in a new way each day.

Use the following readings to feed your faith in the week ahead: John 14, Psalm 91, 1 John 4:9–10. Choose your favorite verse from Psalm 63 to write on a piece of paper and post where you will see it often.

Journal Page

O Lord, You are so

and I am so

Please forgive me for

Help me

Please bless and take care of

Thanks, Lord, for

Abundance

Recognizing and Responding to God in the Midst of His Abundance to Us

(A Study of Psalm 66)

Written by Susan M. Schulz

Edited by Martha Streufert Jander

Editorial assistant: Laura Christian

3558 South Jefferson Avenue, St. Louis, MO 63118-3968
Manufactured in the United States of America

Contents

Session 1

Lydia's Abundance

In this session, we will seek to recognize the many places of God's abundance in our lives. We will examine Lydia's response to God's abundant gifts to her and realize from where our own desire and strength to serve the Lord actually comes.

Begin with prayer. Ask the Holy Spirit to bless your study of His Word so that you grow in the knowledge of God's abundant love and blessing.

Briefly mark and discuss your levels of abundance under "**Where Am I Now?**" Do "**The Search**" to gain a better understanding of God's plan at work in your life. Write your answers in the spaces provided.

"**Respond**" to God's abundance with prayer and praise.

Before the next session, do the "**Do,**" using the journal page and prayer starters following this lesson.

In a few words, describe how you understand the word *abundance.* Then, on the lines below, mark your level of abundance in each area listed.

Material Possessions

- -

Barely Enough   Great Abundance

Physical Health and Strength

- -

Barely Enough   Great Abundance

Free Time

- -

Barely Enough | Great Abundance

Talents

- -

Barely Enough | Great Abundance

The Search

Lydia's Abundance

The apostle Paul was on his second missionary journey. In the early verses of Acts 16, we read that, along with Silas, he had taken the young man Timothy to work with him at spreading the Gospel. After bypassing Mysia, Paul had a vision from God one night as he slept. A man from Macedonia appeared to him, begging him to "come over to Macedonia and help us." At this time, Luke, the author of Acts, joined them ("*we* got ready"), and they eventually entered Philippi. Here they met not the man in the vision but a group of women. Read about that meeting in Acts 16:11–15.

1. Though Lydia was a Gentile, she was a worshiper and believer in God and followed the moral teachings of Scripture. She and other women gathered outside the city for prayer, very likely quite frequently, but especially on the Sabbath. What does this tell you about the kind of person Lydia was? What else can we know about Lydia from these verses? What abundance did Lydia, as a businesswoman, most likely have?

2a. Before Paul's visit, there was one thing that Lydia lacked in spite of her earthly possessions. She did not know her Savior, Jesus. How did Lydia become aware of this lack (verses 13–14)? What part did Paul have in helping her recognize this need?

2b. What is your relationship with God? Do you just know *about* Him? Are you intimately acquainted with His Son, Jesus? Would you like to know Him better? What would help you do that? What part do other people have in helping you fill that need? Or, what part can you have in helping others get to know Jesus better?

3a. Read Psalm 66. Pause after verse 5 to discuss what awesome works of God (done for all people) that Lydia, with her newfound belief in Jesus, might list. Also pause after verse 16 and discuss what Lydia might say regarding what God had done for her.

3b. What has God done for you? Share with one other person (or in the large group) something special that the Lord has done for you within the past week. What effect does this have on you as you tell? What effect does the telling have on the person you tell?

Our Response to God's Abundance

4. When God gave Lydia an abundance that would last into eternity by opening her heart to the Gospel message, He also gave her a willing eagerness to share the abundance of material possessions He had given her. Discuss her response to this opportunity and the source of her willingness to share. Why does God give us opportunities to share?

5a. Look back at your responses to "Where Am I

Now?" Tell about a time that you shared from the abundance God has given you. What did this sharing do for you? What did it do for the receiver?

5b. What praise can you give God now for that opportunity and willingness to share from His abundance to you?

6. Do you feel guilty because you haven't shared as much as you should? because you have hoarded God's gifts to you? because you have chosen not to see someone else's need? Like Lydia, we need the abundant forgiving love of Christ before we have any strength or willingness to use other areas of abundance to serve the Lord. The good news is that God does not wait for us to come to Him or to become perfect in sharing our possessions, time, or talents. He comes to us; brings us to repentance for our selfish hoarding of His abundance; forgives us completely for the sake of Jesus' suffering, death, and resurrection; and makes us new!

Giving out of our abundance is a joyful response to God's love. As we grow in faith and in our relationship to God through regular Bible reading and study, worship, prayer, and the Lord's Supper, *God* will work in us to do what is pleasing to Him. How can knowing this make a difference to you?

Abundance brings praise. Read aloud together Psalm 66:1–4. Use voices that "make His praise glorious!" Take turns with others speaking words of praise for one particular place of abundance that the Lord has given you.

In your closing prayer today, bring any concerns to God's throne that arose from the discussion. Pray for God to open your eyes even more to the places of abundance He has given you. Pray for His strength and grace to see others' needs, and joyfully share with them from your abundance. Include more words of praise, especially for rescuing you from sin. After bringing your petitions to God, lift your hands in praise and speak in unison Psalm 66:19–20: "God has surely listened and heard my voice in prayer. Praise be to God, who has not rejected my prayer or withheld His love from me!"

Do

This week, through daily Bible readings and prayer, ask God to help you become more aware of His abundance to you. Record what you learn on your journal page. Write a prayer thanking God for the abundant gifts He gives you. Do you have earthly wealth? physical well-being? a compassionate heart? Are you a good listener? Are you weak and frail, but abundant in time to pray? Ask God to help you use and share from your abundance.

Complete the prayer starters or leave them blank to be used as needed each day during your devotion time.

Additional Bible readings: Psalm 145; Jeremiah 33:1–9; Romans 1:1–12; and 1 Timothy 6:17–19.

For next week, read through Session 2 and fill in any responses as you like.

Journal Page

O Lord, You are so

and I am so

Please forgive me for

Help me

Please bless and take care of

Thanks, Lord, for

Session 2

Hannah Gives Back to God

In this session, we will grow in understanding of Hannah's joy in returning Samuel to God. We will also uncover Satan's tricks to keep us holding onto God's blessings instead of holding onto God.

Begin with prayer, asking for an abundance of blessing from the Holy Spirit to help you grow in faith as you study God's Holy Word.

Complete the sentences under "**Where Am I Now?**" to check your responses to abundance. As you do "**The Search**," keep in mind God's faithful, forgiving love and rely on His power to increase your faith.

As you discuss ways to "**Respond**" to God's abundance in your life, pray for His direction and strength to follow through.

Before the next session, do the "**Do,**" using the journal pages and prayer starters following this lesson.

Finish the following sentences and discuss your responses:

If I had a million dollars, I would feel …

I would use it to …

If I had one year of free time, I would feel …

I would use it to …

The Search

Hannah's Abundance

1a. For many years, Hannah had grieved because she had no children. She brought her grief to the Lord in His temple and asked Him to remember her and bless her with a son. Hannah promised God that if He would give her a son, she would "give him to the LORD for all the days of his life" (1 Samuel 1:11). Hannah left the temple that day not knowing how God was going to answer her prayer but no longer agonizing in her grief. She was joyful and at peace, confident in God's love for her. God did indeed remember Hannah and blessed her with a son, Samuel. Hannah had received from God the very abundance she had requested. Read 1 Samuel 1:21–28. Write below and discuss what Hannah did with the abundance she received from God.

1b. What have you requested of the Lord lately? How has He answered your prayer? What has been your response to Him?

2a. Now read 1 Samuel 2:1–10, looking especially at verses 1–2. Does it surprise you that Hannah rejoiced as she gave Samuel back to the Lord? Why could she do this? What was the source of her joy? While Hannah rejoiced in the birth of her son, was her response ever directed toward her child?

2b. If Hannah's joy had been focused on the answer to her prayer instead of the God who answered it, she may have been unable to give Samuel back to the Lord. What is the difference in finding our security and joy in the *abundance* God gives and finding it in *God Himself*? How might that difference affect our willingness and joy in sharing His gifts?

Our Abundance

3a. When we hold tightly onto the abundance God gives us, we let go of God. We praise and enjoy His gifts, but forget Him. Does this ever happen to you? How does this affect your relationship with God? What can you do when you realize what you are doing?

3b. Share a time when you realized that earthly possessions and blessings are very fleeting and that your hope, security, and abundance had to be in the Lord.

4. Satan also likes to tempt us to believe that we have worked hard, been good, and in general have earned and deserve the abundance we have. How does modern society help foster this belief? What can this belief do to our willingness to share our abundance with others?

5a. Now read Romans 3:10–18. What do we really deserve from God? Read Psalm 103:8–13 to see what God gives us instead. Why does God give us the abundance, especially salvation through Jesus, we so obviously cannot and have not earned?

5b. How does knowing that any abundance we have is purely a gift from God's faithful love give us a sense of great relief? How does it change what we do with His abundance?

Praise to God

6. Again we see how our abundance is completely God's doing. Again we see that our God is worthy to be praised. Our God deserves *glorious* praise. Keeping your finger at 1 Samuel 2:1–10, read Psalm 66. What are the similarities between Hannah's prayer of praise in 1 Samuel and the psalm?

7. What do these themes of praise and deliverance say to you? How do they apply to your life? What words of praise of your own can you say for God's abundance to you?

Look again at your answers in "Where Am I Now?" How can you use what you *do* have to respond to the abundance you have received from God? (Keep in mind that giving to others is also giving to the Lord.) Finish this statement as well: God has given me the spiritual gift of ______________________________. I will use it to ____.

As you close with prayer today, ask God to help you put your trust in Him, not in the things He gives you. Ask God to let you see His abundance in your life and how He wants you to use it. Pray with and for each other, addressing any concerns shared during this session. After bringing your petitions to God, lift your hands in praise and speak in unison Psalm 66:19–20: "God has surely listened and heard my voice in prayer. Praise be to God, who has not rejected my prayer or withheld His love from me!"

Do

On your journal page this week, write about the ways you enjoy giving back to God from the abundance He has given you. Think in terms of time, talents, and treasures. How do these acts of sharing give you joy? Don't forget to write about the little things like a smile and a friendly greeting, or reading to a child, or cheerfully doing the dishes. Thank God for the ways He is working in your life.

Use the prayer starters each day as you come to the Lord in your quiet time, either writing your own endings to the sentences or leaving them blank to be used in a new way each day.

Devotional readings: 1 Samuel 2:1–11; Psalm 103; 1 Peter 1:1–9. Memorize Psalm 103:1, 5.

For next week, read through the Lesson 4 and fill in any responses as you like.

Journal Page

O Lord, You are so

and I am so

Please forgive me for

Help me

Please bless and take care of

Thanks, Lord, for

Session 3

Hezekiah's Praise

Where Are We Going?

We will examine the wonderful works of God in the life of King Hezekiah and the people of Judah and join with the psalmist in praising God for them. We eagerly anticipate the Spirit's awakening of glorious praise for all that God does in our lives.

Ready, Set, Go

Begin with prayer, asking God to open your eyes and hearts to the abundance of blessings He has given to the church and to you; in particular, the abundant blessings given through His Word.

Fill in the true-and-false blanks under "**Where Am I Now?**" and briefly discuss some of the praise "habits." As you do "**The Search,**" realize again why we praise God and the place of praise in our lives as God's people.

Do the "**Respond,**" enjoying a time together of praise and prayer.

Before the next session, do the "**Do,**" using the journal page and prayer starters following this lesson.

Where Am I Now?

Think about your praise "habits" and mark the following statements true or false.

__ Those around me have to wear ear plugs.
__ I usually praise God only for the really big blessings.
__ God's praise shines in my smile and sings in my heart.
__ I'm afraid to tell of the wonderful things God is doing.
__ Sometimes when I hear the word *praise,* I think, what for?
__ My praise does not show the magnitude of joy in my heart.

Hezekiah's Praise

It has been suggested that Psalm 66 was written by King Hezekiah after God had delivered His people from the Assyrians. This psalm may have been written by another author and inspired by other events, but for the purposes of this session, we will study it in relation to King Hezekiah. Hezekiah, king of Judah, followed the ways of the Lord. Stop here and read what Scripture says about him in 2 Kings 18:5–7.

This spiritual abundance did not mean, however, that there were no troubles in Hezekiah's life. Early in his reign, the Northern Kingdom of Israel fell to Assyria, which had become a cruel and ruthless world empire. Later Assyria captured all the fortified cities of Judah. Even Hezekiah's giving them all the silver from the temple and the royal treasuries, as well as the gold stripped from the doors and doorposts of the temple, did not stop them. Assyria's King Sennacherib sent men to mock Judah's God, placing Him in the same category as the gods of all the other nations he had conquered. King Hezekiah had seen the power and cruelty of the Assyrians. He knew the danger was real. He turned to his God in desperate prayer. Read his prayer in 2 Kings 19:15–19 and God's response in verses 20–23a, 27–36.

1. Read Psalm 66:1–4 and record what King Hezekiah's reaction was to what God did for His people.

2a. In the first 12 verses, the whole congregation joins in praise of the awesome works of God. Why do you suppose the psalmist invites "all the earth" to join in praise to God? What benefits are there to praising God with friends? with the whole congregation? with "all the earth"?

2b. God's great act of deliverance called for a level of praise far more glorious and majestic than the psalmist could give by himself. Share a time in your life when God's actions on your behalf prompted you to ask others to join you in praising God.

3a. Read Psalm 66:5–7. What event is the psalmist recalling here? What "awesome" things did God do for His people in other biblical accounts? Why do you think the psalmist wants worshipers to look again at some of God's works on behalf of people?

3b. What "awesome" things has God done for His church in recent times that you join with others (e.g., in a worship service) in His glorious praise? Why is it important for us to recall God's acts of deliverance for His church today?

4. What happens to our spiritual life when we ignore or refuse to see the awesome things God does for His people? What happens to our praise? What can bring us back "on track"?

Deliverance of a Nation

5a. In verses 8–12 of the psalm, the writer considers again the deliverance God's people have just experienced. List below some of the phrases that describe the extreme danger God's people were in and the phrases used to describe God's rescue.

Danger	Rescue
____________________	____________________
____________________	____________________
____________________	____________________

5b. What dangers face the church today? What words give the same assurance that the psalmist expresses that God can and will rescue His people from enemies today?

A Personal Response

6a. Hezekiah considers God's rescue of His people a personal deliverance as well. In the remaining verses of Psalm 66, he gives his personal response to God. Read verses 13–20. What is Hezekiah looking forward to? What does he want to do?

6b. Look at your responses to question 5a. Share a time when some of the phrases could have described the danger (physical, emotional, spiritual) you were in and God's rescue. When have you or when has someone you know gone through "fire and water" and been brought by God "to a place of abundance"?

6c. What terrible thing did God do to His Son so that He might bring you to a "place of abundance"? Describe that place. How will you let others know about what God has done for you?

Respond

Use the words of Psalm 66 as printed in the following responsive prayer to bring your praises to God. Start out softly and increase in volume. "Let the sound of His praise be heard!"

Leader: Praise our God, O peoples.
Participants: Praise be to God.
Leader: His care for us is bountiful.
Participants: We sing praise to God.
Leader: He sent His Son to live and die for us.
Participants: We say to God, "How awesome are Your deeds!"
Leader: He helps us fight temptation; He forgives our failures.
Participants: We sing the glory of Your name.
Leader: He has prepared a place for us in heaven.
Participants: We shout with joy to God!

Close by praying with and for each other. Include praise for God's mighty works in your lives as shared in the study today. Also bring to God any concerns mentioned. Finally, lift your hands in praise and speak in unison Psalm 66:19–20: "God has surely listened and heard my voice in prayer. Praise be to God, who has not rejected my prayer or withheld His love from me!"

Do

Use the journal page following this lesson to write your own psalm. Begin and end your psalm with a call to praise. In between write about the works of God in your life. Has God rescued you from times of danger? from illness? How has He provided all you need? To what places of abundance has He brought you? Include your rescue from sin and death in Jesus.

Fill in the prayer pages to use in your devotion time this week. Or leave them blank to use in a different way each day. End each prayer time by lifting your hands in praise and speaking Psalm 66:19–20.

Additional readings for the week: Exodus 15:1–21; Hebrews 13:5–6; Luke 2:1–32. Write the words of Psalm 66:20 on a sticky note and put it in a place where you will see it often.

For next week, read through the next lesson and fill in any responses as you like.

Journal Page

O Lord, You are so

and I am so

Please forgive me for

Help me

Please bless and take care of

Thanks, Lord, for

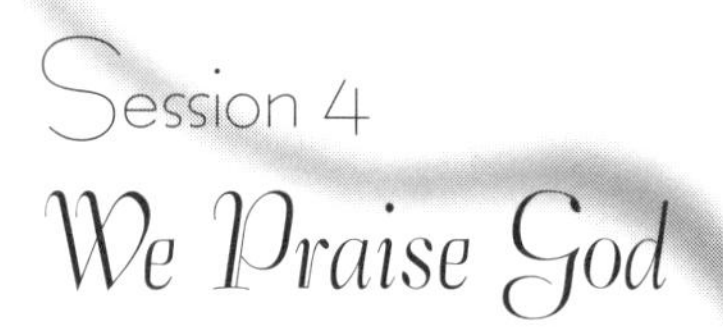

Session 4
We Praise God

Where Are We Going?

In this session, we will bring the picture of God's abundant blessings to life. We will see again how deserving of praise our God really is.

Ready, Set, Go

Begin with prayer, asking God's blessing upon your study so that Psalm 66 will become prayer and praise from your own heart.

Try your hand at illustrating a house of abundance for "**Where Am I Now?**" As you do "**The Search,**" notice the abundance you have in God and in God's name.

"**Respond**" to the blessings of God's abundance with a round-the-table prayer of praise.

May God bless you as you continue regular Bible reading, prayer, journaling, and worship in your walk in God, your source of abundance.

Where Am I Now?

On a blank piece of paper, draw an outline of a large house. Leave space above and below it to add things later in the session. This will represent the abundance God gives. Inside the house, add small symbols to represent specific areas of abundance you have (e.g., coins for material possessions, a heart for love, smiley faces for friends and family, a clock for an abundance of time). Be creative.

The Search

God's Name

1a. Read Psalm 66:1–2. Discuss what it means to "sing the glory of His name." Where does the glory of God's name come from? Write God's name, "I Am," arching over the place of abundance you have drawn.

1b. God's name contains and expresses all that God is. When we sing the glory of His name, we are praising Him for all that He is and does. In the space below, write some of the attributes of God that bring praise to your heart; discuss.

1c. How would you describe glorious praise? Write a few words of such praise.

God's Power

2. Read Psalm 66:3–8. When we see God's deeds and the display of His power, we are awed and react with praise. God's enemies, however, react in a different way—they cringe before Him. Why don't we cringe in the face of God's power? How is God's power a part of our place of abundance? Add a large hand under your drawing to represent God's power.

3a. Verses 6 and 7 talk more about God's power. What significance do the events and truths recorded there hold for us?

3b. Discuss what God has done for His people in the past. What do you think it means that God "rules forever by His power, His eyes watch the nations"? How does this affect your trust in the Lord's place of abundance for you?

3c. Finish this statement: Since God turned the sea into dry land for the children of Israel, I know He can ____ for me.

4. Why should the rebellious not rise up against God?

5. The psalmist's remembering of God's power motivates his call in verse 8 for the sound of God's praise to be *heard*. What happens to a tiny bud of praise when it is expressed out loud? Does it not burst into bloom? Can a bud of praise, never shared, never vocalized, ever burst into *full* bloom? How does vocalizing God's praise enrich our experience of God's abundance? Draw a flower in your house of abundance to represent glorious praise.

God's Help

6a. Read Psalm 66:9–20, then reread verses 10–12. How can God's testing us and allowing us to suffer distress help us understand and desire the true abundance found only in God?

6b. Look at verse 17. Why can we too have praise on our tongues at the same time as we cry out to God in our distress? How does the assurance of God's constant care beautify our place of abundance? Draw a heart around your house to represent God's care and love.

7. Many psalms begin and end with praise to God. Why do you think this is so? What effect can praise at the beginning of your prayer have on your prayer? What effect can praise at the end of your prayer have on your daily life?

Our most important abundance comes from the sacrificial death and resurrection of Jesus. Without that, we would not have access to God through prayer. Without that, we would have no forgiveness or heavenly reward. Without that, the meaning of anything else we consider as "abundance" becomes flat and meaningless. Draw a cross over your entire picture and say together: "Shout with joy to God, all the earth!"

Respond

Read through the entire psalm once more. Look at the place of abundance you have drawn and decorated. Praise God for each gift of abundance represented in your drawing. Take turns with fellow participants praising God; use the following praise starters if you wish:

We sing Your praise, O God, for ________________.
We shout with joy to You, O Lord, for giving us
____.
Praise to You, God, for ________________________.
We rejoice in You, God, for ____________________.
Praise be to God, who has _____________________.

Close with prayer, praying with and for each other. Include any concerns discussed in your session today. After bringing your petitions to God, lift your hands in praise and speak in unison Psalm 66:19–20: "God has surely listened and heard my voice in prayer. Praise be to God, who has not rejected my prayer or withheld His love from me!"

Do

As you write in your journal this week, focus primarily on your spiritual abundance. Think of all you have simply because of your relationship with God. What promises has He made to you in Scripture? What promises have you seen Him fulfill in your daily life? When have you felt His peace, His power, His forgiveness, His undeserved blessings? Rejoice in this spiritual abundance. Look for opportunities to share your abundance with those around you. Remember God's constant, empowering love.

Use the prayer starters each day as you come to the Lord in your quiet time, either writing your own endings to the sentences or leaving them blank to be used in a new way each day.

Use the following for daily devotional readings: Isaiah 41:9–20; 2 Corinthians 1:18–22; Hebrews 8:10–12. Write and display 2 Corinthians 1:20 on a slip of paper.

Journal Page

O Lord, You are so

and I am so

Please forgive me for

Help me

Please bless and take care of

Thanks, Lord, for